Lights Out In the Attic

WRITTEN BY JUDI SCHRAM

ILLUSTRATED BY ELLEN RONTAL

Elliott the husband

Thank you for comi
I certainly hope you
enjoyed my new pl...

♡ Judi

...ng ... for
...detait Love you
Denice

thanks
for enjoying

You're the greatest Beth!
Becky

Don't ever turn your lights out!! :)
Judi

HAve fun growing older! ♡ -Binay

Thanks for supporting my wife!
Brad

Lights Out In The Attic
Copyright ©2015 Judi Schram

ISBN 978-1622-879-41-0 PRINT
ISBN 978-1622-879-42-7 EBOOK

LCCN 2015943990

June 2015

Published and Distributed by
First Edition Design Publishing, Inc.
P.O. Box 20217, Sarasota, FL 34276-3217
www.firsteditiondesignpublishing.com

Dedicated to my cherished cheering section:

My dear husband Brad
My poetry consultant Zack
My tech consultant Justin
My support team Ali and Danny
My sweet sister Linda
My inspiring friend Andi
My dear friend and illustrator Ellen Rontal

A special dedication to my dad, Fred Rapoport,
my biggest supporter and role model

What inspired me to write this book?

While experiencing a life transition, or, more bluntly, a later-than-midlife crisis, I began to write. Ideas and reflections came pouring out of me. One day a poem appeared on the page. Now where did that come from?

I just followed my tapping fingers and a style appeared, inspired by Shel Silverstein poems I used to read to my children. But the subject matter that was manifesting itself was not the fantastical, wildly creative stuff of Silverstein. Rather, it was the "stuff of life" that my friends and I were experiencing, more grounded in reality yet woven with humor. My audience and intent presented themselves: a book for aging boomers, my cohort, with an underlying message of "we are going through this, and the best way to do that is together, and with laughter."

I had so much fun creating this book. My hope is that it brings you joy as well.

Judi Schram

PART ONE
Body Parts

Lights Out in the Attic

My brain is less facile
than it used to be.
I can't find my keys,
and names just escape me.

My car in the parking lot
moves on its own.
Which friend of mine called?
And I can't find my phone!

It's almost as though my
head is full of static.
Is that what they mean by
"Lights Out in the Attic"?

Body Parts

Things creak in the morning.
They collapse late at night.
And all day in between
they just don't work right!

Certain parts ache
(a sore muscle here).
Others parts hurt
(a nerve pinching there).

Eyes that don't see well
while driving at night.
Oh how we long for
our once-perfect sight!

Ears that don't hear well,
what is all that static?
It's the damned hearing aid...
I've really just had it!

But then there's that sunrise,
my sweet sister's smile,
the kiss of my sweetheart,
the laugh of a child.

All body-part failings
(which is how I see 'em),
just fade to the background
as I *carpe diem*.

Cellulite

Help! I'm being overtaken by cellulite,
cellulite, cellulite.
I'm being overtaken by cellulite
and I don't like it one bit.

Oh no,
it's on my toe.

I'm rankled,
it's up to my ankle.

Oh geez,
it got to my knees.

Please advise,
it's all over my thighs.

Oh flumox,
it invaded my stomach.

I'm alarmed,
it took over my arms.

Oh dreck,
it crept up my neck.

Oh dread,
is it really on my forehead????

The Middle

When we were six
our body parts
were just where they were meant to be.

At sixteen years
some parts grew bigger
(they said it was part of maturity).

When twenty-six,
as we had children,
some parts grew huge and smaller again.

By thirty-six
things settled back in
and landed sorta where they had been.

At forty-six
we worked very hard
to keep parts where they belonged.

Then fifty-six
parts kept on moving.
We felt like we were wronged!

Now sixty-six
gravity takes charge.
Our body becomes like a riddle.

Parts that were high
are low, low, even lower.
But most end up in the middle!

Bathing Suit Shopping

I'd rather have my tooth pulled
or a colonoscopy,
than shop for a bathing suit.
It's worse than torture to me.

I walk right by the bikinis,
straight to the one-piece rack.
Can't even look at tankinis.
I need a potato sack!

Chinny Chin Chin

Once upon a time
adorning my face
was a chiseled chin
in just the right place.

One day I woke up
and gazed in the mirror,
thought I saw double
and had to look nearer.

Is that a shadow?
Perhaps a mirage?
What's that tumescence
upon my visage?

Is this a joke?
Not one chin, but two?
And it is sagging.
Can this be true?

I tried contouring,
thought of surgery.
A few months later,
I woke up with three!!

Hairy

What is that hair
on our chinny chin chins?
It doesn't belong on our faces.

Why do these hairs
pop up on us
in all of these unwanted places?

Then there's that one
growing out of my mole
right in the middle
of my cheek.

I'm really afraid
I look like a witch,
or some great hairy
monster freak.

Why is that hair
sticking out of my nose?
I truly do look scary.

My mom didn't warn me
about all this stuff.
When did I get so hairy???

The Stripe

While brushing my teeth this morning,
I glanced into the mirror
and there I saw the dreaded stripe!
I blinked to see it clearer.

That stripe of gray upon my head,
adjacent to the scalp.
I'd better call the Red Salon.
I must have Nathan's help!

Nathan is a magician.
I need to keep him near.
His best trick is the one that
makes the stripe disappear.

Another trick that's up his sleeve
is taking frizz away.
Nathan, please move in with me
and do my hair every day!

Bad Hair Day

A cowlick here,
a cowlick there,
and frizziness
all through my hair.

Kinky on top,
looks like a mop.
I really can't
go anywhere!

I look so bad,
I see some gray.
I have to fix it,
can't delay.

I iron the side
to make it flat.
Oh, give it up...
put on a hat!

Victoria's Secret Models

Are those models for real?
Not an ounce of fat.
Are we the same species?
I never looked like that!

But I need a new bra,
so I'm off to the mall...
Victoria's Secret.
They've got a lot of gall!

I don't see a department
for hot grandmothers like me.
Nothing that's appropriate
for someone over fifty.

I have to go to Nordstrom
to the plus-size department.
I need to lift my boobs up,
and keep 'em in separate compartments.

Those models should be locked up,
and never on TV.
They're not good for the mental health
of women like you and me!

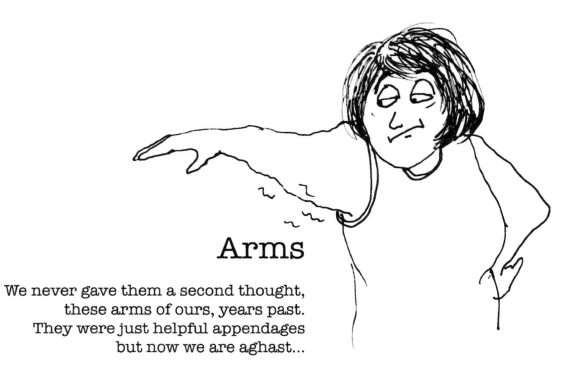

Arms

We never gave them a second thought,
these arms of ours, years past.
They were just helpful appendages
but now we are aghast...

each time we put a t-shirt on,
a sleeveless dress or top.
What is that crepey texture there?
This really has to stop!

This transformation of our skin,
and let's not talk elbows!
We need a new accessory
like arm Spanx or arm hose.

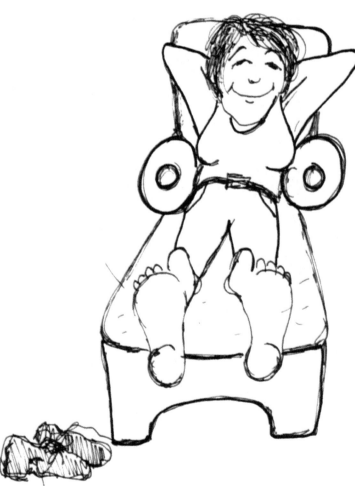

Best Foot Forward

I'd love to put my best foot forward
but besides veins that are varicose,
my left foot has two bunions
and both feet have several hammertoes!

I used to love my three-inch heels
now coated with dust on my top shelf.
They made me look so tall and slim
(at least that's what I told myself).

Thank god for Naturalizer shoes
with their hip and trendy styles.
I pretend that they're Manolas
and stroll around for miles.

Menopause

My sweater's on,
my sweater's off.
The sweat is dripping
from my nose.
The red blush that
crept up my neck
just flushed my cheeks;
That's how it goes.
These hot flashes are not much fun.
They hit you when you least expect them.
I'm trying to take them in my stride.
I honestly detest them!

But someday soon
they'll go away.
Tomorrow would be
fine with me.
One body temp
all day and night
is preferable
to twenty-three!

The Night Owl

Once upon a midnight dreary, while I pondered weak and weary,
over kids' ungrateful moanings and some long-forgotten chore...
as I nodded, nearly sleeping,
suddenly there came a bleating,
comprehensively defeating any chance of sleeping more.
"Oh, not again," I muttered, "why'd I leave the Ambien at the store?"
Quoth the husband,

"SNORE"

Gotta Go

I gotta go.
I really can't wait.
Why do I always
end up in this state?

Just got to Whole Foods...
don't really have time.
Gotta go before I get
to the checkout line.

If I don't heed Mother Nature
and get to the bathroom quickly,
we will hear a voice announce:

"CLEAN UP AISLE THREE!"

Nighttime Activity

All is quiet, deep in sleep
when peace is suddenly shattered.
Oh my goodness, not again...
not my stupid bladder!

These bathroom antics have to stop.
I deal with daytime disruptions...
But really? Through the night as well?
I can't afford these interruptions.

I'm desperate for my beauty sleep!
My husband understands my plight.
That's who I see in the bathroom hall...
        night after sleepness night.

Make Up

THEN

A pinch on the cheeks,
real quick, on the go,
was all I once needed
to get a fresh glow.

NOW

My make-up regime
could take a whole hour.
And still those brow lines
will make me look dour.

I WILL persevere...
I'll erase those eye rings.
I will line my lips...
(if I could just find those things)!

Sizes

You'd think my closet was a store
and not my own collection.

One could actually shop in there
and have a varied selection.

Not just of colors, trends and styles,
but of sizes 4 through 12.

Truth be told, I've worn them all
(not that I am proud of myself).

It'd be nice, and quite a bit cheaper,
if I could stay one size,

and 6's filled my closet
(with a few 8's and 10's as standbys).

Spanx

Lift it up.
Smooth it out.
Hide the lumps and bumps.

This invention's
the very best thing that
ever befell rumps.

White pants?
No problem!
They look fantastic now.

Tight dress?
No issue.
I won't look like a cow.

And to whom do I owe
a great deal of thanks?
I don't know her name
but she invented Spanx!!!

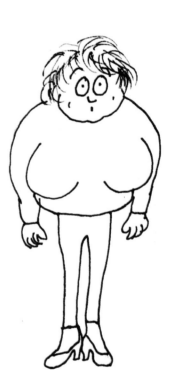

Too Old

What am I doing on this ski slope?
The runs are labeled black or blue.
Those are the colors my body will be
when my risky descent is through.

What am I doing on this bike?
The one with thirty gears.
One gear is enough for me.
I'll break my neck, I fear.

What am I doing on this mountain trail?
The steep one that I just traversed,
sweating, tripping, gasping for air.
And now I must go down in reverse!

I'm too old for all of this...
pushing my limits, finding my edge.
I need to get a back massage,
then lay around and veg.

A Glimpse Into the Future?

A friend and I sat down to eat
at our favorite place to dine.
We ordered soup and salmon salad
and garnished with a glass of wine.

"Look," I sighed, "at those old women,
sitting right across from here."
"That'll be us," she groaned gloomily,
"in ten or maybe fifteen years."

"Oh my goodness," I proclaimed.
I looked a little nearer.
"That isn't two old strangers there,

WE'RE LOOKING IN A MIRROR!"

Magic Eraser

If I had a magic eraser,
you know what I would do?
I'd erase the wrinkles on my face
and all the age spots, too.

I'd erase the veins
upon my legs
(the ones that are unsightly).

I think I'd do this
every morn,
and even do it nightly.

If I had a magic eraser
you know what I **should** do?
Erase the frown upon my face
and be happy for each day with you.

PART TWO

Memory
(or lack of)

Glasses

I know I put my glasses here.
I saw them yesterday.
This is infuriating.
I need them right away.

I'm nearsighted and also have
severe astigmatism.
The world without my glasses
is like looking through a prism.

I've looked high, I've looked low.
I've even looked beneath my bed.
Please help me find my glasses.
Oh! Here they are.
Upon my head!

The Word War

It is there, just out of reach,
that word I'm trying to find.
It's buried in my frontal lobe.
I'm going out of my mind!

You know that thing we use sometimes
to strain the noodles we have boiled,
or rinse off fruits and vegetables?
Now I'm really getting roiled.

Ok...I'll go from a to z
and try to ply it from my brain.
I hope it doesn't start with z
or I will surely go insane.

The a's don't work, nor do the b's
and when I think that I've just had it,
I get to c and it feels right.
A word pops out from all the static....

It's "colander"! I'm so relieved!
Another tiny battle won.
At least until an hour from now,
because the word war is not done.

Where Is My Cell Phone?

I'm talking to my sister Linda
while getting ready for the day.
Suddenly frantic, I start to panic
and barely manage to say,

"I'm in such a hurry
and now I can't find my cell!"
"What?" says my sister,
"look in your hand!"

I'd better lay down for a spell.

I Hope I Didn't Throw It Out

Where is:

My checkbook,
my i-Phone,
my glasses,
my purse?

My earrings,
my wallet,
the remote?
What a curse!

I'm so dismayed that I could shout.
(I hope I didn't throw them out!)

Names

I know the face,
she looks the same.
I know the face,
just not her name!

It could be Joan,
or Nan or Sue.
I really haven't
got a clue.

O.K., I'll use my technique now
and scan straight through the alphabet.
I hope it helps me with her name,
and then I pray I won't forget!

What Am I Doing Here?

I was heading for my bedroom
'cause I had to start to pack,
but when I passed the kitchen,
I whipped up a little snack.

I saw a stack of clothes
in the laundry room.
I threw in a load of darks
and then I grabbed the broom.

I began to sweep the back hall,
garage and pantry, too.
Re-entered through the front door
into the living room.

I dusted the brick hearth
and watered wilting flowers,
when I realized
that I forgot to shower.

I went back to my bedroom
and as I entered I cried,
**"I know I was heading here before.
I know I was...
BUT WHY?"**

Home From the Market

Oh my god! What's wrong with me?
I can't believe I did it again.
I bought another peanut butter.
That brings the number up to ten.

And ketchup? The one I bought
will nestle very nicely
between the six already stored.
The condiments enticed me.

While in that aisle I also bought
some onion powder and garlic salt,
both of which I now can see
I've several of...it is my fault.

I never remember what I already have
so I always seem to slip up.
Dinner tonight is onion and garlic,
peanut-flavored chicken with ketchup.

(oops...I forgot to buy the chicken)

Big Trouble

I think I'm in big trouble and
right now I'm really stressed.
Though I couldn't think of names and such,
at least I could get dressed.

I reached a brand-new low today!
At work I sat to read the news.
I crossed my legs, looked down and saw
on my feet...two different shoes!

PART THREE

Weight, Diets and Exercise

Healthy Food

Sugar-free

Sodium-free

Gluten-free

Dairy-free

Nut-free

Trans-fat-free

Cholesterol-free

Calorie-free

Flavor-free

One Pound, Two Pounds

One pound,
two pounds,
three pounds,
four.

This weight gain
is killing me.
I've never
weighed more.

My pants are tight.
My blouse won't button.
I really must stop
being a glutton.

But that's okay,
because it's Sunday.
We all know diets
start on Monday!

Cravings

Salty or sweet?
I can't decide,
while into my pantry I gaze.

Chips or a cookie,
or maybe some nuts?
Perhaps I will just graze.

But then there is
the fridge as well.
The freezer offers more.

Must not forget
the treasure trove
that lies within those drawers.

I know there is
some ice cream there.
Some chocolate or strawberry.

I even think
I have a pint
of fudgy Ben and Jerry's.

Oh my god,
should I walk away?
Can I summon my willpower?

Salty or sweet?
I think I'd better
just take a long cold shower!

The Scale

I shouldn't have bought that stupid scale.
I think it must have been on sale.

But there it sits on my bathroom floor.
I can't ignore it anymore.

First I take off all my clothes.
Then I get on...all ten toes.

What is this? It can't be right.
Must be the salty food last night.

Or else this lying scale is busted.
I'll take it back, it can't be trusted!

I'll give it away, it'll be a mitzvah.
I'm hungry now...
let's go get pizza!

Diets

Atkins
The Zone
South Beach
Master Cleanse
Mediterranean
Beverly Hills
Weight Watchers
Nutrisystem
Skinny Bitch
Macrobiotic
Jenny Craig
Glycemic Index
Starving

I'm not going to try to make all of these rhyme.
Just know that I've tried every one...
TIME AFTER TIME.

Exercise

Why do all my friends
like to exercise?
Many of them do
to stay a small size.

Others are addicted
and highly motivated
to stay in good heart health.
So why do I hate it?

It's hard and it's painful!
I end up full of sweat.
I just don't feel the "high"
that others seem to get.

I feel all sore and achy
by the next morning.
And a sharp chest pain
attacks me without warning.

"No pain, no gain," I hear them say,
I can't believe that's true.
It shouldn't be excruciating
for benefits to accrue.

But then I read statistics
and I've come to realize
there may indeed be credence to
the merits of hard exercise.

So I'll try some yoga,
Pilates and brisk walking.
I've exhausted my excuses.
I've done enough balking.

I'll start tomorrow. Yes I will!
Tomorrow I will hustle.
I hope I make it through the day
without pulling a muscle.

No Time

I planned to take Pilates.
The class begins at noon.
BUT
I need a mani-pedi.
I'd better get there soon.

I paid up for a series
of step-aerobics class.
BUT
I need to get a hem done
so I think I'd better pass.

I signed up for Vinyasa.
The class begins at seven.
BUT
I need some Diet Snapple.
Off to Seven-Eleven.

You say these are excuses?
Not true, you're telling lies!
It's just that I'm so busy
I've no time to exercise!

Yoga

Down dog is the posture.
You lift up your ass.
What am I doing
in this damn yoga class?

They say it's my core
that I'm trying to strengthen,
and muscles so tight
that I'm trying to lengthen.

This room is so hot,
is that really necessary?
I sweat enough, thank you.
(God, my legs look so hairy!)

And in "forward fold"
when I am bent over,
the skin on my knees
looks like my Shar Pei Rover.

How many more minutes
till I get to shavasana?
Then I can meet you and
and go out to lunch with ya.

PART FOUR

Doctors

Doctors

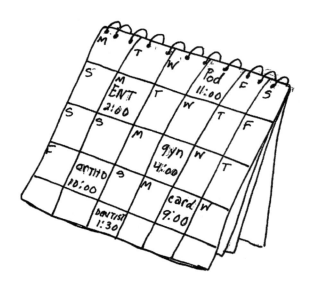

My calendar was once filled
with productive, fun endeavors,
like yoga and art classes.
I read novels and knit sweaters.

But now my days are filled with
a different activity;
schlepping from doctor to doctor,
all over this fair city.

From orthopod to ENT
to my podiatrist.
From primary doc to pain doc
and cardiologist.

Let's not forget the chiro,
GI and gynecologist.
I know I'm forgetting someone...
so I'm off to the neurologist!

The Adjustment

Crack goes my back.
Oh heck, it's my neck
that's making that funny sound.

I'm down on the table
and really not able
to turn my head around.

Dr. Fixx insists
that these painful twists
and distressing manipulation

will cure my sciatica...
but I gotta tell ya

I just need a long vacation!

The Prescription

After watching the commercials
for the little purple pill,
I heard from Dr. Gutterman
who said "You're not that ill.

"You have a moderate case of
gastrointestinal reflux.
Here's a scrip for Nexium,
sorry to say, it costs a few bucks.

"I'm not sure if it's covered,
but I hope you will be fine."
I drove straight to the Walgreen's,
and got to the front of the line.

The clerk looked up the paperwork
and said, "Don't be distressed.
This costs 500 dollars."
My heart leapt from my chest.

So in addition to the reflux,
my naive drugstore trip
caused major cardiac issues.
Now I need another scrip!

The Mammogram

That damn prescription stares at me
displayed upon my desk.
I need to have a mammogram,
a process I detest.

Do I have to do it
every year or every two?
The research is confusing.
I don't know what to do.

I schedule, then I worry
as the day grows near.
The morning of the appointment
I'm overcome by fear.

I pick up *People* magazine
in the waiting room.
I try to stay distracted
from my sense of doom.

I know all the statistics.
I try to stay upbeat,
but it is so difficult...
I tremble in my seat.

And then I hear my name called.
I approach the X-ray center.
The very scary monster machine
confronts me as I enter.

The hard cold gleaming metal
clamps down upon my breast.
"This simply can't end soon enough,"
I think as my chest is pressed.

And then the brutal wait
for the test result.
She comes in with good news:
Don't even need a consult!

Now I can repress this
for another year,
or is it two or five?
It's still so damn unclear!

The Derm

Remember when the derm

mostly picked your pimple?

Or maybe took that mole off,

the one right near your dimple?

These days our derms we do adore

because they can do so much more.

They are, I bet, our favorite docs.

Why? They make magic with Botox...

and with those fillers like Restalyn.

If only they could make us thin!

Visit to the Plastic Surgeon

"Hi, I'm Dr. Mann.
Let's see what we have here.
You came in for a tummy tuck,
I'm looking at your rear.

"There is a great procedure
that lifts your butt like in Brazil.
You'll have the best butt in the room,
not going near a treadmill.

"To balance out your body,
which is a surgeon's goal,
your breasts should be much larger.
They'll look great in a camisole.

"And since you will be under,
you will hardly feel a thing.
So how about a facelift?"

What's he thinking?

Ka-Ching!

PART FIVE

Technology

Too Many Buttons

Too many buttons and too many switches.
The more complex the mechanics,
the higher chance of glitches.

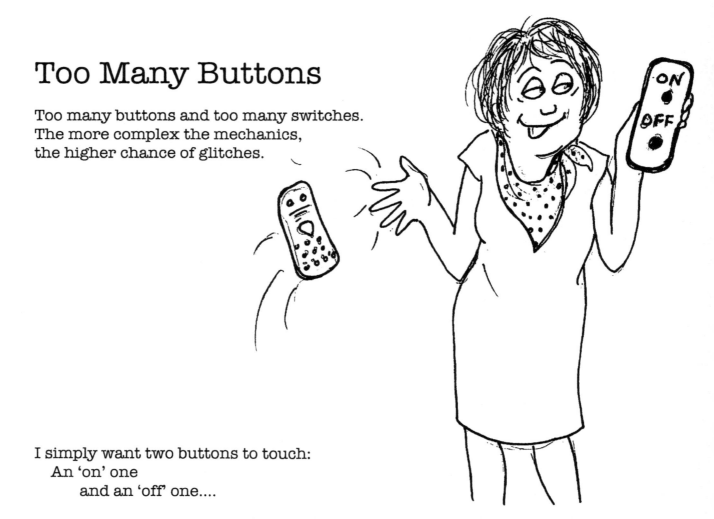

I simply want two buttons to touch:
    An 'on' one
        and an 'off' one....

IS THAT ASKING TOO MUCH?

Tech Impaired

T A P

T O U C H

T A G

T W E E T

Not sure what they mean
but I won't admit defeat.

I will try hard to learn
the meaning of these terms,

and become a lot more techy
so my kids won't disrespect me.

Computeritis

I'm really sick, it's serious...
I think I have a virus.
I caught it from my computer;
I have computeritis.

The symptoms are annoying:
cut-and-paste confusion,
achy file attachments
and file-saving dissolution.

Even more alarming
are dysfunctional deletions,
upload/download disturbance
and black inkjet excretions.

The saying about an apple a day
simply doesn't apply here.
My Apple is causing my illness
and I need a doctor (or engineer)!

Help!

I picture someone sitting there,
a devious sort of person,
conjuring up sadistic ways
to make my workday worsen.

A technological person,
in charge of techie things,
who is intent on making sure
my life's more challenging.

He creates online systems
that are impossible
for any human to decode.
It is extremely cruel.

I need help! I need it now!
Will someone be so kind
to please come by and rescue me?

(BefoRe I LoSe My Mind!)

The Phone Call

I have to make a call today
to get phone service back.
I paid my bill,
I know I did.
I paid it! That's a fact!

I have to use my office phone
to dial the company.
You know the one I'm talking about:
AT&T.

For "Balance" push the number one,
for "Sales and Upgrades" two.
For "Billing" try the number three.
Four gets a new phone for you.

And now we're on to number five.
It is the "Voicemail Helpline."
Six will get you "Tech Support."
(I think that it goes up to nine.)

The most amazing fact of all,
the most incredible thing:
an hour has passed and I have not
spoken to a human being!

I stay on for an eternity
and finally get redirected.
I'm so excited, I'm almost there!
And then...
   I'M DISCONNECTED!!!

Texting

I tried to send a text to you
but every time I tapped the "i"
the "o" popped up and messed me up
and I got "ho" instead of "hi."

This texting stuff is really hard.
If God had meant for us to do it,
he would've fashioned tapered fingers.
A better way? I wish I knew it!

Facebook

Many are addicted,
forget to work and play.
Accomplish nothing else
while on Facebook all day.

Reading fallacious rants
that people share...why?
And lots of silly minutia
that's just plain TMI!

You had a colonoscopy?
You can't find parking spaces?
I think that we should all be on
a need-to-know basis!
BUT
on the other hand,
it's nice to stay connected.
Sometimes old relationships
may be resurrected.

It's nice to know your cousin Joe
has gotten out of jail.
FYI: my daughter Kate
just got her first choice, Yale.

Although I've fought the impulse
(I tend to resist trends)
I s'pose I may
sign up today
and join with all my friends.

Siri

I have a new friend Siri.
She's now a part of my life.
She is supposed to help me
but she causes me such strife!

I ask for information
when I need a hand.
But oftentimes
she says to me
"I do not understand."

I ask her to connect me
to my best friend Andi,
but she says some other name
Like Brad, or Stan or Sandy.

And then there are directions.
On her I have depended.
For sure I'll end up somewhere,
but not where I intended!

So Siri...

If you want to stay my friend,
you really better shape up.
Or I'll never call you and
if you call me, I'll hang up!

Infomercials

In the wee hours of the morning
(or the middle of the night),
my eyes are heavy-lidded
but won't close, try as I might.

I turn the television on.
I toss and turn in bed.
I hope that I will drift to sleep
but snap awake instead.

"Squeeze your way to thinner thighs,"
I hear my old friend Suzanne say.
I could use that, so I tune in....
"Get your credit card right away!"

Now I'm at my full attention.
Now my senses are so keen.
I keep watching and I'm sure
I need the "Power of OxiClean."

"But wait there's more," a person shouts,
"we'll throw in a rotisserie!
And if you call us right away
you just might double your money!"

Perhaps I need some spray-on hair,
or Ginsu knives for my flank steak.
I'd love a Power Juicer.
Think of the smoothies I could make!

As dawn approaches, my credit card
is just about all maxed out.
I start to fade, but jolt upright;
I need a Snuggie, there is no doubt!

Telemarketer

We started eating our salad
at a quiet dinner for two,
when the phone intruded loudly.
I didn't know what to do.

Should I answer or should I not?
It was a true conundrum.
It might be something crucial,
like a good friend with a problem.

It could be my sister Linda,
my son or my granddaughter.
I answered the irksome phone.
It was a telemarketer!

To make matters even worse
it was a robocall.
Need to lower your interest rate?
No I don't...not at all!!!!!

Our meals are much more peaceful now.
We get to cookies and tea
without much interruption.

THANK GOD FOR CALLER ID!

63

Passwords

There are too many to remember
and whenever I forget,
my online life is stymied and
I'm riddled with regret.

Why didn't I write it down...
record it in my note section?
Or file it under contacts?
So now I cannot function.

They say create new password.
I dread all that confusion.
When will I learn? I must control
this damn password profusion.

iLove

Match, Christian Mingle, Cupid and JDate.
Even farmers have a website
to help find a soulmate.

Facebook, LinkedIn, MySpace, Google Plus.
Social media's exploding.
What is all this fuss?

Twitter and Tumblr, Pinterest, Flickr.
Do we need to share everything?
Can life move any quicker?

Call me old-fashioned.
I yearn for the past.
We met in a bar,
or maybe in class.

Any yet....

However, it happens
whatever the website,
the goal is well worth it:
find Mr. or Ms. Right.

PART SIX

Friends

Modern Communication

Four people at a restaurant
circa 1980,
could be found interacting
and communicating.

Flash forward to today
at exactly the same place.
All four are also talking
and sitting face-to-face.

But look a little closer
and you'll be able to tell
they're not speaking to each other...
they're talking on their cell!

Or perhaps some are texting.
It really doesn't matter.
I miss the good old days
of interactive chatter.

What if I suggested
in a manner most polite
that all phones during mealtimes
should be off and out of sight?

I suppose that's unrealistic,
an outright fantasy.
What will likely happen is
no one will invite me!

Posing

My good friends all assembled
for a special birthday dinner.
We lined up for a photo op.
Oh god, I must look thinner!

I move to the middle and turn sideways,
then put my hands upon my hips.
I jut out my chin to remove the double
and slightly purse my lips...

so as to downplay my deep laugh lines...
I'm getting in a bad mood.
Let's get this over with...I am so stiff
and ready for my food!

At the Restaurant

I'd like to order lunch, I say,
I am extremely hungry today.

I think I'd like to have the Greek,
but please withhold the onion and beet.

I'd also like some well-done fries,
and put the dressing on the side.

I'll have some toast without the butter.
What is that you say? What did you mutter?

You think I am a pain?
I'm driving you insane?

Well, I must say that really does hurt.
But wait until I order dessert!

Desserts

"Would you ladies like dessert?"
our waitress Sandy queries.
"We have bread pudding, créme brûlée
and ice cream with fresh berries."

"What? No chocolate?" I exclaim
and Sandy's full cheeks redden,
"Oh yes" she cries, "of course there is;
dense chocolate cake with almond."

We each wanted a different thing
and in the old days would've
all ordered to our hearts' delight
and maybe we just should've.

Instead, with honed restraint I said
(more accurately, I whined),
"One piece of cake with four forks please,
and hurry before I change my mind."

Gossip

Did you hear 'bout Joyce and Stan?
I think they're separated.
I don't want to dish the dirt
because I really hate it...

but I thought that you should know,
and now that we are talking,
have you seen Jane's bad facelift?
It really is so shocking!

I do have some exciting news;
It's nice to share that, too.
Janie's daughter Jenn is pregnant
not with one, but two.

What? You say that Sue's been spreading
stories about me?
Of all the nerve! I can't believe
that she's so gossipy!

Can't Play Mahj Today

I cannot play Mah Jongg today,
said grumpy Judi Schwartzberg-Kaye.

My arthritis started acting up.
I have a bad case of hiccups.

My blood pressure is through the roof.
I think I have a decayed tooth.

An aura is boding a bad migraine
and down my neck is a shooting pain.

A blast from the past is tennis elbow.
And just this morning I stubbed my toe.

I think I may have fractured my wrist.
My hearing aid is on the fritz.

My fibromyalgia is back again.
I feel like the flu's about to begin.

And don't even let me tell ya
about my damn sciatica.

My bad knee is...what?

What's that you say?
Bitchy Marilyn is in Del Ray?

Ok, I'm coming by to play!

It Takes a Village

Remember that movie with what's-her-name?
Divorced, she was back in the dating game?

C'mon, you know, she was blonde, kinda pretty.
At first all we felt was sadness and pity

but then she got stronger, and started to feel
liberated, empowered, her heart and soul healed.

"I think her name begins with a 'd,'
Karen piped in, "or maybe a 'c.'"

"I remember a painting...something like that,"
Nanci intoned, "then she found her own flat."

"In New York?" queried Andi, deep in her thoughts,
"she walked in one night and her husband got caught

cheating on her...jeez...what was her name?
It starts with a 'j,' like Janice or Jane."

"It's Jill!" exclaimed Bev, "Jill Clayburgh!" screamed Sue,
"I think I just thought of the movie's name, too....

"An Unmarried Woman"!

The torture could end.

It **does** take a village.

Thank god I have friends.

Only Your
Best Friend

Only your best friend will tell you when:

Your shirt is unbuttoned,
your pants are unzipped,
a booger's in your nose,
and your t-shirt is ripped.

There's spinach in your teeth,
and toilet paper on your shoe.
What would we do without best friends?
What would I do without you?

PART SEVEN

Marriage

The Remote

There are so many choices
CNN, CNBC.
Thank god the remote
makes it much easier for me...

to switch back and forth,
from substance to fluff.
Must try to stay current,
but love all that stuff.

"Say Yes to the Dress"
and HGTV
have a place right beside
MSNBC.

Now let's not discuss
remote wars with our spouse.
That's why we must have
two TVs in the house.

Man Cave

There is a place
I dare not go,
although it's in my home.

You'd think it were
top secret,
a "no admittance" zone.

I'm not sure what
goes on in there.
It's guarded like some forts.

But mostly,
from what I hear,
it's got to do with sports.

Deafening noises
of chants and cheers
with an occasional roar.

Ear-splitting shrieks
and moans and groans
escape beneath the door.

There is a place
I dare not go,
although it's down the hall.

I told my husband
I understand....

AND TOOK OFF FOR THE MALL!

What?

"Hey, what are you doing honey?"
   "No, I don't have any money."

"Please get me at four."
   "You fell on the floor?"

"I think I lost my new black coat."
   "You're starting to get a bad sore throat?"

"You need to go to the E.N.T."
   "I wish that you'd stop yelling at me!"

Patience

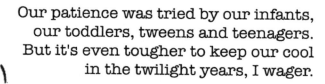

Our patience was tried by our infants,
our toddlers, tweens and teenagers.
But it's even tougher to keep our cool
in the twilight years, I wager.

When your hubby can't hear a thing,
because of presbycusis,
and your throat is sore from screaming,
you just might blow some fuses.

When your wife can't see a thing
due to a cataract condition,
and she banged into your Buick,
you have to repress some aggression.

Patience is a virtue, we know.
We learned it as young children.
We'll have to count to ten again

(and then go take our Valium).

Bedtime

My eyelids are drooping.
It's been a long day.
I crawl into bed.
My thoughts slip away.

I roll to my left.
I see probing eyes
as he reaches over
to stroke my right thigh.

This would be foreplay,
there is no mistake.
Now the dilemma...
will I partake?

It has been a while,
yet I whisper in his ear,
"I love you so much,

But not tonight, dear."

I Remember

Her

I remember when my hubby
had hair upon his head.
When did my love get chubby
and start to snore in bed?

I remember when his muscles
used to bulge beneath his shirt.
And when all through our dinner dates
he used to flatter and to flirt.

Him

I remember when my sweetie
had thick long brunette hair.
Her figure was so gorgeous
and her skin was smooth and fair.

I remember when she danced,
she was so lithe and limber.
She used to tempt and tease me.
Oh yes, I do remember.

And though time has changed us,
of one thing I am sure;
as we traverse the years to come,
our great love will endure.

PART EIGHT

Family

Forever Mothers

She glares at me with those big brown eyes.
Her disdain for me is undisguised.
"I'm twenty-eight years old," she mutters.
"Don't care," I say...

"I'M STILL YOUR MOTHER!"

Moms and Dads

What do moms do?
Worry.

What do dads do?
Watch sports.

Our Children

Emerge from our bodies.
Fill up our hearts.
Occupy our souls.
And then they must part...

create their own lives,
separate from ours.
We're Mother Earth,
but they are the stars.

Empty Nesting

The rooms that were once filled
with homework, clothes and toys
are now empty, not a soul,
no more tumult, no more noise.

No more children in the house,
just my husband Brad and me.
Not even a dog or a cat
to keep us company.

Do we walk around naked?
(I'm just a bit too fat.)
Do we make love all day?
Really, who has time for that?

You miss your kids, but then you can
rediscover your husband/your wife.
Empty nesting ain't all that bad.
It's another chapter in the "Book of Life."

Waiting

My friends all have some grandchildren,
many have two or three.
It sometimes feels like everyone does.
Everyone but me.

My husband and I are waiting,
there's nothing we can do.
My friends all say "your turn will come."
I'm not so sure it's true.

"But wait," my husband Bradley quips,
"We can't pull off abduction.
Let's find a special agency
for grandparent adoption.

Or better yet, let's
dim the lights and get into the mood.
We can start trying on our own."

Now isn't he so shrewd?

Joyful Noise

While empty nesting,
the quiet surround
was truly appreciated.

But then there seemed
to be a void
and the gratefulness abated.

Something was missing.
Something was lost.
There was a lack of noise.

What were we wanting?
What were we craving?
The sound of a child's voice.

And then there was you.
You entered our lives
and became the central part.

Your joyful noise
filled up the void
and also filled our hearts.

Early Childhood

I finally finished decorating,
expressing my aesthetic.
But then I was turned upside down.
Okay, I've gone and said it!

I'm admitting I was upset
when I moved the furniture,
and hid all my accessories **BUT**
I would do ANYTHING for her.

My precious little Sophie,
I'll empty my house if I should.
Instead of "Early American"
my house is "Early Childhood."

Car Seats

I know car seats are crucial.
We used them with our kids.
But now the way they make them
could make you flip your lid!

There's this strap and this other.
I can't figure how it goes.
I finally think I have it...
Oops, it's tangled in his toes!

Child Proof

There's a lock under my sink
and a gate across the stair.
It is impossible
to get from here to there.

You may surmise the reason:
My grandson stays with me
each Monday, Wednesday, Friday.
They're crucial for his safety.

But then there is that issue
of trying to get my pills.
I twist, I turn, I tweak my wrist.
I'm sure you know the drill.

We go to such excessive lengths
in trying to protect our youth.
Do we have to go SO far?

Does **EVERYTHING** have to be child proof?!?!

Quality Time?

"Can you please watch Max for me,
tomorrow until two?
I have to go to work
and my sitter has the flu."

"Of course, I'd be delighted,"
I said wholeheartedly.
"You can even take more time.
I have at least till three."

Max arrived at nine o'clock.
We played a rousing round
of Hungry Hippos for a while.
Then I heard that sound...

the bleeps and pings and buzzers
are noises that I know.
They're sound effects emitted from
"Angry Birds Go."

"I don't want to nag you
and be so annoying,
but can you please take your nose
out of that thing?

Let's play a game together,
how 'bout Connect Four?"
"Not now, Gramma, later...
I need a higher score."

So for the next few hours,
to avoid a big blowup,
I watched Max play on that darn thing
till his mother showed up!

Sandwich Generation

I love my parents,
I love my kids,
and I am in the middle.

Figuring out how to balance it all
is really quite a riddle.

My kids have kids
so that compounds
my predicament.

How can I be
two places at once?
I just need to vent.

Babysit till twelve o'clock.
Take Dad to doc at one.
Take Mom to beauty shop at three.
I must be there for everyone.

I love my parents,
I love my kids,
and I am also a wife.

But...

I know how lucky I truly am
to have these people in my life.

Full Circle

They were always there for us
through all of our transitions;
No matter what the challenge was,
we were their precious children.

To care for, to love,
to nurture, to support.
Their strength and good counsel
steered us to safe port.

The years have flown by
and taken their toll.
Although quite insidious,
we've now reversed roles.

Now we're there for them,
through their life transition
toward their twilight years;
it's no imposition...

but done with great love.
Indeed, we are grateful
that we're here to help;
now life's come full circle.

EPILOGUE

Retirement

I once had a career.
It challenged and fulfilled.
I had a good, long run,
devoted right until...

I finally retired
(after fifty years).
I decided it was time,
despite my many fears.

I feared I'd lose my self worth,
my identity.
Would I still know who I was?
Would I still know me?

Well, I've had my moments,
some periods of strife.
But now I'm happy writing
this next chapter of my life.

Boomers

Born between '46 and '64?
Then you are one of us.
We are the baby boomers;
older, yes...but ageless.

We are not succumbing
to the throes of Father Time.
We're fighting back with all our might,
staying in our prime.

We are the best educated.
We accumulate degrees.
High school is just the start;
on to masters' and PhDs.

We were known as spoiled brats
but now we're working longer.
Self absorbed? Perhaps.
But we made the economy stronger.

We're known as the "I" generation
but that has morphed into
The iPhone, iPad and iPod,
and epic medical breakthroughs.

We're focused on improving the world
at a dizzying speed.
Microchips and superconductors...
we are the space-age breed.

Our inventions range from high tech:
GPS, seat warmers, and flat screens
to the more mundane and vain:
discreet bifocals and relaxed-fit jeans.

Yes, we were the activists,
we questioned everything.
It allowed us to reimagine
to reinvent, to dream...

dream of possibilities
for our daughters and our sons,
for the world that we will pass on
to future generations.

Judi Schram's "Book of Life" has had several chapters:

Chapter I: **Growing up**
Grew up in Detroit, Michigan, and its surrounding suburbs.

Chapter II: **Education**
Attended the University of Michigan, graduating with a Master's in Speech Pathology.

Chapter III: **Professional Life**
Worked as a speech pathologist specializing in early childhood speech and language disorders for thirty years.

Chapter IV: **Personal Life**
Married childhood sweetheart Brad, and had three children, now adults.

Chapter V: **Professional Volunteer**
Worked as a full-time professional volunteer in various capacities.

Chapter VI: **Now What?????**
Fulfilling passions she didn't even know she had: writing and making people laugh.

Ellen Rontal

Born March 15, 1951, Ann Arbor, Michigan

B.F.A. University of Michigan School of Art and Design 1973

Scholarship Banff Center of Fine Arts, Alberta, Canada 1973

Designer Visual Concepts 1973-1975

Founder of Yucks greeting cards 1980; Free-lance artist for Carolyn Bean greeting cards

Co-owner Mesa Arts 1984-1999

Children Folk Art portraitist; illustrator and cartoonist

CPSIA information can be obtained at www.ICGtesting.com
Printed in the USA
LVOW05s1910180815

450620LV00006B/6/P